The

Case

Against

Happiness

The
Case
Against
Happiness

Jean-Paul Pecqueur

ALICE JAMES BOOKS

FARMINGTON, MAINE

10 9 8 7 6 5 4 3 2 1

Alice James Books are published by
Alice James Poetry Cooperative, Inc.,
an affiliate of the University of Maine at Farmington.

ALICE JAMES BOOKS
238 MAIN STREET
FARMINGTON, ME 04938

www.alicejamesbooks.org

Library of Congress Cataloging-in-Publication Data

Pecqueur, Jean-Paul, 1968-
The case against happiness / Jean-Paul Pecqueur.
p. cm.
Poems.
ISBN-13: 978-1-882295-59-3 (alk. paper)
ISBN-10: 1-882295-59-5 (alk. paper)
I. Title.
PS3616.E286C37 2006
811'.6--dc22
2006023698

Alice James Books gratefully acknowledges support from the University
of Maine at Farmington and the National Endowment for the Arts. ❦

Cover art: Robert Bechtle, detail from "Hoover Man (man With
Vacuum Cleaner)," 1966, lithograph, 52.4 x 37.9 cm,
courtesy Gallery Paule Anglim.

Acknowledgments ⎯⎯⎯⎯

Grateful acknowledgment is made to the editors of the journals in which these poems first appeared (sometimes in slightly different forms):

American Letters and Commentary: "Matthew Confronts the Very Air"
Arts and Letters: "There Must Be Some Kind of Way Out of Here"
Columbia Poetry Review: "Feeling Occidental," "Like an Avant-garde
    Classic in Braille"
Lit: "Patty Suddenly"
Passages North: "Third Degree of Heaven"
Quarterly West: "Second Hand"
River City: "On Wasting Time"
Seattle Review: "Truth"
Sonora Review: "Howell Street Apartments"
Spork: "How to Make the Case Against Happiness," "Let's Go,"
    "To Start Again," "What We Want When We Want It,"
    "Yellow Birds"
Verse: "The Beekeeper's Apprentice," "He Who Would Know
    Art Must First Feel at His Ease"
ZYZZYVA: "Long Distance Communication," "Discord at
    the Cartesian Theater"

"Diary of a Seducer" was also previously published by David Kirschenbaum as *Boogcard #12*, in conjunction with a reading at The Poetry Project.

    I would like to thank my teachers David Marr, Harriet Linkin, Richard Kenney and Heather McHugh for demonstrating what poetry is and what it can do. Thanks to Joanna Fuhrman, Derek Sheffield, Rene Keep, Maggie Golston, and Mark Horosky for keeping the conversation alive and vital. To Kazim, April and the rest of the Alices—many thanks for all your help, but most of all for letting me play. And special thanks to Judy Hendren, whose love and support has been immeasurable.

For Patty

Contents

And it was not precisely
Happiness we promised
Ourselves;

We say happiness, happiness and are not
Satisfied.

—GEORGE OPPEN, *Of Being Numerous*

        . . . thence may I select
Sorrow that is not sorrow, but delight;
And miserable love that is not pain
To hear of, for the glory that redounds
Therefrom to human kind and what we are.

—WILLIAM WORDSWORTH, *The Prelude*

Truth

The door to the Center for Educational Renewal is never open.
This is not a metaphor.
Other doors in the corridor are left ajar
in perpetuity,
their entries backlit like so many afterlives.

I watch as a man in khaki shorts and a pale green sweater,
his infant son secured to his back, steps
through one into the sound of male laughter,
as through another rushes a pale, angular woman.

She hurries toward the east exit,
the static rap of her heels
mixing with the story of a student
loitering just outside the Center's door.

The ratio here refers to the name of the good guy,
the student appeals to her taciturn friend,
intimating that hers would be an ethical narrative

if only the ideal audience could be found,
an audience who would know implicitly

exactly how it matters that we can be mistaken
about what we think and what we feel.

To Start Again

Before tackling the actual infinite
etherized into some cliché of blue,
you should practice with the difficult moment,
the heirloom crystal serving platter
shattered in a baroque fit. You might reflect
upon why you sent the letter riddled
with precision machine buzz and thorns.
Maybe it was because of an absent mother?
Decorative shadow on the dining room wall?
At first the invisible is tangible
only when it's rotten with technique,
so daily exercise your technique
as though the great guest house were on fire,
which it is, the house of uppercased Being
being consumed while you sit reading
thinking fretting planning and Big River
follows its clumsy course to the sea.
Stupid lugubrious stupid myopic river,
the heart is made of sturdier stuff
than that Neoplatonic sweetness and light.
Admit it. On hundreds of occasions
you've tried to piece it all back together
only to discover some hissing swan
or vaguely swan-shaped piece missing,
and still you feel you'll be made whole again.

To Get It Right

My barber has read *The Aeschylus*
five times during the past year.
To get it right, he says.
Of course the irony's easy.
The character of any one man
fashioned, like fame,
from bravado and accident
is another man's mood,
or fate. So when the shop's
only other client, a tan, slack–
chinned architect, says take
my son, he recently moved
to Venus (his words) you know
that city like a body with canals
for veins and all that art,
and I suggest that arteries
might prove a more useful,
if not more precise,
metaphor, I am brushed off,
but I don't mind because
I too have studied the tragics
and profess a like sentiment,
a kind of negative golden rule
where you don't do wrong
so no bad wrong's done you.

Long Distance Communication

When my mom calls late Friday to say
she found the stereo's remote control hidden
in the hallway closet under one of Murphy's
favorite western shirts, the one whose mother-
of-pearl buttons stand out from the turquoise
rayon like a hermit thrush in a clearing,
what she wants to say is that the old blue
dog is sick, will probably die soon, with
or without her help, and that she's tired
of living all alone like a minor character
from some plot-bare English novel who learns
thirty years too late that security is really
a bad pun on a polysyllabic Greek word
forever lost when some inquisitors decided
the best idea would be to burn Alexandria.

There are sentences with no appropriate context.
What I mean is that my mind is an informal entity,
multidirectional as light. Then there are sentences
where the arrow equals its mark. The man
in the second row exclaimed that he expected
the remote control to return, but he really meant
that if I insist on pulling the proverbial sword
off the axiomatic mantel, I'd better have a plan
for wounding someone. But those are sentences
too heavy for even two healthy bodies to shoulder,
so Mom continues to explain how the shirt
didn't even fit him when he was most alive,
rail-thin from splitting wood all day in the snow,

but how it's pleasant to have around anyway,
why must we forget everything we ever loved.

Just as when the instructor said to his class
that Pound warned us to go in fear of abstraction,
what he meant was pain: a broken façade, a charred
beam, a lone tie tack. Last week I received a note
from my friend telling me he'd two months to go
at his current assignment, that the smoke
had mostly cleared, that his emotional life
was finally a blessing. But all I heard was that
there had been a fire, all number of structures
going up like genetically engineered blooms, and
that he was caught creeping around the heroic dark
with a five-gallon bucket of gasoline
and half a box of strike-anywhere matches.

There Must Be Some
Kind of Way Out of Here

Thus to be let down, but gently,
easily, as one more leaf aloft
on one more autumn breeze,
one more riotous cascade of hair
on dog day's plush backseat becomes
the regulation fantasy of release:
there must be some kind of way out of here.
How else can you explain the decadent
flourishes of the expressive
and abstract movements, the right angle's
stubborn blue or flounced, multifaceted
cherub. And what else is art,

other than a clever way to demonstrate how,
created as it was before escape clause,
safety net or gold became standard,
the human being's leading problem,
its most tangible opposition, has always
been the indispensable burden
of body. Death is no small affair.
Only it feels so fucking good,
as Ginsberg might have taunted,
to disappear upon the rocky shore
of a sob or expire like spermatozoa
in the last gasp's momentous effulgence.

But try selling this to a woman
whose nerves and muscles are misconnecting
like a joke under water,

a woman who will not lift her gaze
from the daisy-patterned photo album
filled with snapshots of a face
she never saw fit to see clearly;
try asking her where to prop the drained head,
what exit strategy for the poor, rueful beast,
and she will likely say that sometimes
it is best to weep first, then look.

Authority Complex

When the authorities advised us
to test drive the future
before committing to any long-term plan,
the very first thing I did
was to rush off in search of a badassed ride,

but the only transport I could find
was this rusted out, third-rate muscle car,
a not quite legal American junker
sunk in the septic field
of a drunken friend's yard.

Little did I, or any of us, know
that those who would sell us tickets out
were really just purchasing
advance tickets for their own returns,

that such is the wage of authority,
the base price of ground floor entry
into the polite quarters of society
where good citizens preserve their personalities
as though they were extinct, cannibalistic birds,

or that one day I would be sorely tempted
to accept just such a salary,
to haul my boyhood, that bloodied wreck,

out of memory's weed-choked backlot
into the parts yard of a domestic history,

to survey the damage, take account,
then clean it all up for a neat display
behind which I would stand, pronouncing
to all who visit: *I hope you found
what you were looking for. Thanks again.*

On the Way from Delphi

I thought it was to be a lesson, something
you do, and then are done with:
as in, I have already done
the Three Modes of Truth, or Keats,
or please, just call me if you need
to work late, you know how I worry.

And even though I do not know,
have never really known, drifting
through days as though through cold
spectral flames, my hair curled,
my skin smelling one moment of cedar,
the next moment of cedar-flavored smoke,

and therefore am, like a precocious child,
constantly asking myself why
the dwarf irises have been yanked
from their snug beds, why those stars,
why this lacquered sky, that tedious
expanse of fuzzy muzzy nothing;

yes, even though the span between objective
and act is most often impassable,
I must believe joy is not impossible.
This morning, hours before the sun
began its sluggish crawl over the *Rincons*,
a small handful of shoppers converged

near the long rows of empty carts
in the mega-market's shadowy,

air-conditioned cavern of an entry
to watch a teenaged Chicana
practice cheers in the surveillance camera.
I can't explain it.

No one knew what we were cheering for
yet this didn't seem to matter
as if just inside those pneumatic doors,
once removed from the shallow lights
bordering the dormant parking lots,
we fleetingly became the actors we loved.

Hollywood West

Great acting and crying on cue
are not the same thing.
Aristotle must have had this in mind
when he revised pathos
from *that which happens to*
to *of the soul, emotion, passion.*

Such audience awareness was surely
an early, primitive stab at the test–
marketed ending—all the good boys
escaped alive, but the queen was left stranded,
the prince all squirrelly, the young hero
lost in his love of a popper and bubbles.

Which brings us, finally, to Julie Andrews
whose tripping across the Alps has become,
as Frank remarked, the perfect metaphor
for symbolism, keeping in mind that
all else being human, one may as well learn
to fabricate promising, profitable crises.

For F&M

Garden Variety Apology

I feel it has little to do with pleasure.
The woodpecker guzzling nectar
from the tear-shaped hummingbird feeder,
my eyes raw after a day in the sun,
day turned to shadow. I turn it over

in my mind until it disappears,
replaced by the latest installment
of this hour's news
broadcast like salvation
by my freedom-loving neighbor.

It seems he has found an answer,
and so stands there spraying bottle
after family-sized bottle
of earth-scorching petrochemical
into his ten square feet of garden-slash-yard.

If only *I* could try so hard, I think;
there are so many things I cannot say
which are precisely those things
I know must be said, but

with the warplanes overhead,
and all the uproar that just won't stop,
from keening machinery
shooting through the arteries of this city
toward its desiccated heart,

to that part about getting and spending
as symptomatic of rotten and spent,

the part about too long pent
in the low grey furrows of the brain
one loses touch, and then,

which returns us to now,
on this stifling spring evening,
even if I felt like trying
I wouldn't know what to say at all.

Survival of the Fittest

I want to say that I do not know
what brings us here
nor what keeps us indoors
under these harsh, accusatorial lights,

but I've got this sinking feeling.
The young red-haired guy on the stool beside me,
he's been fuming for hours
about how he lost his latest job

because when he digs a trench goddammit
he doesn't wanna hafta fill it in again,
which his partner, a thin-lipped man
in an implausibly bad brown suit,

thinks is damn straight.
And what is life anyway, he erupts,
but one continual labor of uncovery?
To which I want to say that I do not know

but he has the morning paper
and its leading headline screams:
"Seven More Bodies Found
Buried in Accused Killer's Backyard."

Outside the bar, the off-white and badlands-
pink strip malls spread
like a preprogrammed crime spree
while the partner continues his dreary countdown:

Dozens of teenaged goons with American guns
and wet dreams, ha-ha, of fields full
of hundred dollar bills, boys really, yesterday
they soiled themselves with their neighbors' blood.

Can you believe that?
Yes.
Yes I can believe that.

The Only Justice Is Love

This morning, driving
through dense waves of sterile
bone-bleaching desert air,
aimless as a repeated mistake,

I swear I felt the globe revolving,
throwing its dying weight around
like a sperm whale in a tidal pool,
spawning some unfathomable suffering.

What was it that I had expected?
A sudden reversal?
To shed my skin and emerge radiant,
all gain with no remainder?

On the radio, a blonde voice
was methodically enumerating
the most recent tragedies
to befall some representative village—

more nightmare than paradise—
first drought, then typhoon
bringing down mountains of mud
with a new strain of flesh-eating virus.

Gathering fresh fuel for my daily outrage,
I listened with dreadful glee. Then,
in a rare neural burst, a thought:

Though I'm not ready to love myself,
the only real justice is love.
Just the one burst of some chemical
not quite eternal. And that was it.

II

Yellow Birds

At first, wanting everything to feel all romantic,
I memorized a handful of the, quote,
immortal words of the eternal Shelley,
suspecting that there was something to his
each poor passing moment is
a rare and delightful beauty. So sue me.
No, really. It felt like a season
of floating the shallows submerged
in the tenure of dreamless sleep. Cool,
that is, like a chill pill. Later
I just flailed and sobbed and screamed
what have I done with my goddamn keys?
Thinking, that's a pretty funny gesture.
Or not. When I slip into that night,
what do you think stares tellingly back?
A tongue-tied marionette spot welded
to some Jr. administrator's gilded age?
Or history personalized as gone astray
in a Jersey-sized thicket of how-to books
fencing out even vaster forests of dream
and need? For two lazy decades
dialectics of loss seemed just the thing.
Now military software shadow boxes
with every third tank-like car. Where
oh where leads artlessly to my oh
my Ohio, that Lebanon of the pastoral
scheme. Ever been there? Me neither.
Ever seen a live one? Yep, me too,
and I'm still paying for it, spitting bits
of faulty teeth into the offering plate

while the morning's chainsaw chorus
chirps oh take me back to the backyard
garden's potted delight where the house
sparrows squawk at the house finches
as the goldfinch flutters and cries. Wait!
I know that dance. I pull my pants on
one leg at a time. Give me a minute.
Okay. I can show you those ropes now.

How to Make the
Case Against Happiness

Offer it a bribe. Say, Happiness
why don't we take the chill ease
of this spring day and make something special,
you and I, some demiurgic cocktail
to sip as the sirens plunge
over the edge of our private peso opera.

The future adores its hometown parades,
the donkeys on bikes trailing flies.
Biting flies. Fireflies. Suggest fireflies.

Say, Happiness, I sure like you more
now that you're no longer a bio-
morphic reserve
in the developmental leagues—nice cut,
but no turd in the parlor.

The enthusiast's dream is a rapt idol,
an escape module fashioned like a second head
from government surplus neoprene.

Describe one bird you have never seen.
Show it to Happiness. Say, Happiness
these balloons are seized by razor wire
while yonder burgles a mortgaged wind.
We'll give you one chance to make it swing.

Howell Street Apartments

The man in apartment 3D owns a hamster
which thinks itself a squirrel. The man
thinks of himself first as a pianist. Of course
the harpsichord thinks differently, as do Sundays
trimmed with those heavy metronomic plinkings.
From time to time Bud reproduces documents
to make us think he is an emissary from Canada.
Everyone loves the Canadians: the Canadians
are so civilized; so comely. Think of Ottawa,
we say, where if a critical mistake is made,
the ministers file it under pitfall and slip off
to buy creamy boysenberry milkshakes. I too love
a creamy boysenberry milkshake, but one Friday
last week someone threw a switch in Bud's foyer.
The additional weight upset the sacramental Koi
which sank like garish medallions in the claw-foot tub.
Never was seen such a thrashing before.
The hamster became uneasy. He thought
he knew what would happen next. Another sign.
The man had renamed his utopia Catskill,
which he pronounced as though he really had spent
the better part of his youth overseas. Overseas,
ah! that lovely country where one often witnesses
wee critters moved about as if they were counters
in some limitless game, sort of like the way
we used to play, during love, with the first third
of the official version of the standard,
western metaphysical lexicon: Being/Non-Being.

Feeling Occidental

The word ontology, the monopattern
of shadow on a north-facing
roof, the sphere's thrice-
figured density, the remainder
of zero (chimera of clarity) exist
in the particular material and sensitive
instruments, the micro- and stereo-
scope, the sentence which begins I,
the undersigned, the undersigned
and his family, your family,
the brother sterile and wed
to the futures market, the aunt
poisoned at birth by a bee
sting, a pin-prick, an accidental,
afternoon, fall-down
vision, by a tiny sliver
of sentience—have you
ever felt it, that just
accusation, the exact
tongue, the exact
finger tip.

Closer to Home

The idea was to exude words
like pheromones
salts or attitude then
to abstract from these a style
as painfully immediate
as a land mine or
closer to home cocaine
cut with leaded glass
and Drano or possibly
two styles one
for the days when the heart
feels faint as the mouse
gray chalk gray rain falling
in an anonymous mid
western land
scape painting and one
for those moments
the split seconds
the afters

On Wasting Time

The figure could be described as in repose
in the same way that men are said to be in love
or actions in vain, each swelling to fill its abstract,
ill-conceived element, air or other, with novel strains,
forms harmonious, as waves would fill an ear.
One need only glance at him encamped there, pausing
to rest, a stylized dragon on the sea's vast blue verge;
head lolling, trunk and tail undulous as the psychedelic standards
of this, the dawning of the 4696th year of fate imperturbable,
to hear we've got joy, joy, joy, joy down in our hearts sweep
across the breeze as though whistled lightly, almost trippingly,
by eager young beach-combers. The beach wears such thick,
luxurious hair. It appears so emphatically Epicurean
you might think I'm addressing you from some chichi salon
rather than my shallow-hulled bark. You may even say
that I have shut my eyes to the frost on the chokecherry
and the white, white sky and so have lost my way.
Please do. The psychology's not difficult. Prepositions tend,
Rene reminds me, to render positions necessary. I'm thinking
of John Locke again who, having long meditated upon the war
of all against all, resolved the stand to take on wasting time
was directly abreast the body, parallel to the vital organs.
From here one could best aim to strike the decisive blow.
He set all this down in his *Second Treatise*
of Government, an otherwise unremarkable book,
briefly summarized: spolia victori; or, the pre-dawn robin,
his hymn the worm who planned, ideally, and became what it was.
I repeat ideally here because every relation requires a minimal
degree of idealization. Steep just one moment more trilled kettle
to tepid tea. Jasmine for luck. Orange for prosperity.

And though a stern habit is to be preferred to some longing tumultuous then cool, one should not seethe all the time. Thus other positions to assume on wasting time are: horizontal, level, fixed, or flush. Prostrate, prone, or supine. Recumbent. Flat as a pancake, a board, a flounder or a prairie. Concave. Incurved. Hollow or depressed.

Enthusiasms Are to Research
as Day Is to the Sublime

because they impose upon the desertscape
an anti-honorific qua transitory hue

because the stars are filled with entertainment news

because throughout the news the people flow

past the garden and alarm factories

past the sparrows and Sibeliuses
the motorcycles knife-fighting in the yard

past the tree cosseted with mockingbird charms

because the tree in question is the tree of life

because the tree in question has grown out its hair
the scent of orange blossom is everywhere

04-07-04

Tucson's Classic Rock

which scary dude, quoth Maggie
which judgment legislating for feeling
on which watched and worn-out corner

in the slowly draining light of June
        the palmetto frond
                is a roach scaling the wall

in Tucson

in June the wind smells of creosote
it smells of ozone and of trouble
but you get used to it, quoth Maggie

as in—it becomes you
like an old habit of blackish-blue skirts
it becomes the music you move to

Tucson's classic rock
fuck you, screamed from a passing car
please, oh please, whispered in reply

Black Capsules Like a Spaceman

When I was young I used to be able to sing just like Donna Summer, but then something happened to me. On TV I saw the boiled junkies. They were melting MacArthur park with their foot-long butane lighters. Wash, wash, wash your head, the shampoo commercial said. But I was trapped outside the screen where watch was all I could do. So I folded, packed myself into a shoebox called "your room." It was years before the news leaked through. *Some diseases are guaranteed to make your menace more beautiful.* It seemed like a promise, that plot to plant millions of civic roses in the atmosphere, so I hurriedly began germinating my own carnivorous rose by entering black capsules like a spaceman. Now I am a free citizen and float most weeknights in the fog-light of my unfurnished apartment, randomly deploying nanotechnologies modeled on the electric guitar and remaindered primal scream therapy. Need I say that I feel proud, so awfully proud?

Or Some Such Remarkable Idea

The scene panned as I'd often expected,
effect-wise, but my feelings no word,
that moment, could auger. Jan exchanged
her twelve geldings for the pony carousel
and a year of lariat instruction. She had wearied
of anniversaries, of versifying cowhands
afeared of success. Obstacles holding back
our joy ought, she avowed, to be profound
like hula hoops of fire. Eric agreed. He had
for nine months been shamefacedly plugging
the millionaires' club. To hear him recite,
over whisky sours, the Mademoiselle Jr. article
which advanced the modern male entrepreneur
as a delicious fantasy of exile was downright
beautiful. It ultimately moved me to tears which
I soon enough discovered was the vacant plot
nearest to goodbye in our fashionable community.
Not that they were overjoyed to be rid of me;
only, having once chosen requited love, or some
such remarkable idea, they felt I was better off
alone with my thoughts, one and two and. . . my
forlorn sliver of English garden and mimosa sutra.
And so it was there, some weeks later, beside pie-
eyed peony, that I first saw the young caterer pull up,
his Mustang purring like a Sister of Mercy.
He smiled, and I whispered back, and you must then,
dearest Joan, understand why I was not nonplussed
when the vegetable vendor arrived already red-handed.

Death Shall Not Define Us

Lately it seems that everybody
wants to talk about the duende,
the fluttering like a torn leaf
or grubby old childhood sheet
frayed by incident and surrender.

For instance, last week at the mall
a salesclerk in Bachman's Shoes
tells me, as he's lacing a pair
of coffee-with-cream oxfords,
that the song playing on the radio,

a muzaked version of *The Way
We Were*, has always reminded him
of how everyone must die.
So then why, I wanted to ask,
don't we just pack our bags and go,

but I didn't dare, seeing
that he too knew what it felt like
to want nothing more
than to swallow the future whole
like a little black pill.

Instead, I tried to lighten the air
by assuming my favorite pose,
that of the ridiculous man thinking

in his pinkish-white sport shirt
and new, unreasonable shoes.

There are those who say that death
is the definitive insult
in a world puffed-up by insult,
but I say death shall not define us.
Two bony, raw-eyed security

warily circled the open sales floor
as though measuring a cage.
Their tags read Angie and John.
The young salesclerk, his name is Don,
as in the coming light of, as in tomorrow's.

What We Want When We Want It

The bumper sticker on my friend's car
reads Visualize Whirled Peas
so I close my eyes and concentrate.
But all I can see through the grey snow
of dead ocular cells is me suspended
over my desk with its clutter of photos,
last month's letters and party bubbles,
my eyes screwed shut. It seems
I am trying to concentrate, but the day
keeps casting me out, reeling me in.
Fill the thistle sock for the goldfinch.
Water the lava rocks. First coordinate,
then subordinate. If what you don't know
cannot hurt you, then it must be impossible
to be hurt by anything at all, which sounds,
on the whole, like a pretty fine idea.
Like fifty-one push-ups before coffee.
Like quote-end-quote Now. Now,
just place the needle in the groove,
the groove in the basket. Asked
what I wanted for my birthday.
Asked when I would finish the job.
Asked about the comma, the mocha,
the jaw pain which last week was chronic
today is mostly tragicomic, function
mimicking form like Matisse's *Dance*
where all seems union, more free and perfect,
and bright levitation in the presence of flowers.
Asked where I wanted her to place the flowers
I responded that everywhere would be fine.

Patty Suddenly

then suddenly Patty not.
There were engines in the wings
then the noise receded,
drawing with it the racetracks
and hat racks and my Delaware
oh so unaware. I was the not-
for-profit sighing society
fussing about the central authority
before one day Patty suddenly
then suddenly Patty not.
The day was hot. The year was 1989.
The modern age was sinking
into the parched soil of the Po-Mo world.
Fantastical things were growing.
Glowing breathing tubes for one.
Intolerance for intolerance.
A damned dodgy, doggy-dog world,
for decades, every time I awoke
it was morning—How Boring!—
until suddenly Patty suddenly
then suddenly Patty not!

Second Hand

I was never sure just when she meant
     by all the time in the world.
It seemed the sort of puzzle
     a fledgling Pyrrho might construct
in proof of a theory:
     all relations are untimely.
Love, what sound does the clock make
     not ticking/not ticking?

Outside the theater, stars
     were flickering out like sparks thrown
by a fountain burning in a whirlwind.
     Inside a phone rings
through a large room lit by a bucket
     of ice. Shoe string. Polo
pony. Silver charm. So finite
     are the ways these poor things end.

So disconcerting. On the one hand,
     you can train for decades
to perfect the timing
     for working yourself up
like a funnel cloud, gradually widening
     the expanse of your appetites
to include blood oranges and thumb screws,
     a golden bull, golden

mountains, but then comes the morning
     when the alarm is broken
and you sleep through the counseling session

which is the other hand,
the twenty-seven-boned mammalian hand,
the hand it is best not to show
until the escape route has been planned
and actors paid to light the way.

Let's Go

Patty wants me to write a poem titled
"Poem in Homage to this Poem" mostly
because it has always been about love with her,

about needing to explain away the obvious with her
by reference to the slightly more obvious—
hunger and its descending call notes,
fire's recourse to flame.

With her it's all let's go to the store let's go to the movies
    all the time.
It's all round and round in some Rorschach's pond
of spontaneous intent
like free-falling in an empathic elevator.

If she wasn't at work right now I would need to invent her.
If the stores ran out of sugar,
if the bees abandoned their hives,
if I wasn't teaching right now I'd surely call her.

The classroom's been set on fire, I'd say.
Someone spilt sun all over the desert.
I've this pain in my neck that aches like seltzer.
Let's go and see about those shoes.

Third Degree of Heaven

In the worm's heaven, the sky arcs
like a polar bear's first rib. A little soil.
A little murky water. All the birds yoked
and muzzled. The heaven of carbon,
of comeuppance. And yea
though a rich man may own the copyright
he owns not heaven. This logic
is registered in the angels' daybook.

For me, heaven's a metonymy
where the cosmos plays part
to ego's whole. Ash trees
line the street outside my window
like so many torched cigarettes.
See the problem? Which is heavier,
an inch of heaven or an ounce of lead?

Like so many butt-ends. And the bear
cannot locate his private heaven
because he cannot tell the difference between their
and there. In one myth, there's a heaven of ball
and a heaven of stuffed chairs;
between them cuts a four-lane highway.
It is the middle road, the good road out.
In the other myth, I'm in heaven is a sentiment
proper only to a certified gourmand.

Enter Here

I want to invent a mistake, a punk
rock showcase like Oddbody Hall,
witless as the ear of the absolute.
I want one brute lute to bake with.
A brick toaster oven. Mourning
doves in the yard. I want nary a worry
and just once an owl-topped cairn.
I want that painter's eye in a cup.
More pie, of course. And more
inner resources on monthly lease.
I want it live at five at first but it ought
to look a bit at ease with baloney
neo-pragmatic theses. And why not?
Whose price isn't pegged to death,
that night in which all crows are black?
I want a refund on the decaf break.
It whinnies like a powdered thug. Then,
when the spirit calls collect
on the land line, I want to be transferred
to the idiot owner of this mind-fuck operation:
Who precisely said what, I want to say.
I can't do anything with these words,
and yes, the sandwiches are heavier than air.

We've Been There. Done That.

Most say darkness is a common symbol
meaning we cannot see our way clearly.
And this is supposed to get us somewhere,
to throw open some skygate, backdrop some cue.

They seem so sure of this I no longer know
just where I stand. Under what division
of the blue moon did Empedocles die
that I can hear a sad song and conclude

the radio is feeling la–la–la lonely?
And can you blame me?
I've met machines designed to measure
the heart rate of the wingbeat of the dying

luna moth, machines guided by inner lights
projected from alphabetic satellites.
They were sleek and hairless post-human machines.
Meaning, forget about the Great Chain of Being.

Forget about the woegriefgloom of forgetting.
We are not links broken off Orion's silver belt.
We've been there. Done that. We've boarded ships
piloting themselves across oceans portioned out

to the last molecule just as we have daytripped
over the sunburst the bountiful plains. So go ahead,
tell me again; say something I don't already know
or couldn't just as easily find out the hard way.

April Tercets

There's an exercise of history in the room.
Its eyes are crossed, swollen with X's.
It cannot lift its head off the floor.

It was the same for that poor mute bird,
recurrence, last winter's war orphan,
when he was asked to pick one moment

from amongst the forked monuments,
those memories of the memories of
flowering like parti-colored pageants.

— · —

Same look. Same yawn. Same story.
The sun draws up a milky day
without contour or perspective.

You can see it with your eyes closed:
white bleeding into white like a chip
of shell in a cracked porcelain cup.

Or like a page in place of the window.
Or a likeness of windows of grass.
Who affords such proper arrangements?

It's like planning to witness that one moment
when nothing sort of resembles itself
the way a nightmare reassembles the day

from the memories of ex'ed precedents:
things pouring from hollows, from eyes—
edged things with ochre, ochre things edged—

as though there must be a single perspective
from which to see this would be to see ourselves
plainly as almost equal to a triumphant history.

But whose uniform would we be wearing?
Whose standard raise? Over which address?
And which voice to deliver the memorial cadenza?

In the room there are four blank walls
and a door: a scored desk, oak chair, old books.
The door's open. The books have been opened,

and tonight shall appear a marigold moon;
but today, one moment ago, the sun was outside
and a hot breeze rolled through the ironwood trees.

At that corner where sky seeps
through the thick, chalk-yellow light
I see birds. I see dirt brown

flecked with soft grayish-brown,
finely narrowed slots for song. We carry
their late-hour in-the-airness about us,

an aura mostly incidental, erotomachic,
like the shudder of symmetry, of trees
lining the route from nowhere to known.

April arrives patterned like a question
we must cut the future down to fit.
Could this once have been a new way to think?

To think I asked once again if April,
if the empty mind rattles on the windy plain,
to think of differentiating that white again.

The sun does not advance over the walls.
You can feel it with your eyes opened.
These are not windows to look through.

The Case Against Happiness

Our local painter discovered Paul Klee.
He's the line that marries profit and loss
to those children of our rocky coast,
hair perfumed with the stuff of grief.
The local dentist thinks a tree is a tree's
a tree. Baker refuses to discourse at all.
He calls this pragmatism. I call Patty
but Patty's never home. Wants to stay.
Wants to call it quits. I do too. I want
to say to Happiness, Happiness, if the mind
of the man on the so-called street of dreams
meets, will the day drop off its clothes again,
its dirty, dirty laundry. Our walls, brief walks,
lie down with stunted and alien trees.
Animals, we eat the very air they breathe.

Discord at the Cartesian Theater

Of how it came to be
that we can do what we like,
mostly, yet cannot know what we like
until we set the reconnaissance dinghy adrift
upon the quarry pond of a fully rationalized desire
you insist that we cannot profitably speak.

And yet you have seen what follows: the cow
path meandering across the great divide
with great gangs of bored thrill seekers
rambling on about how there must be a beeline
to Sublime Overlook, or at least a nearby
clear-cut which is not a clear-cut by virtue
of its being a wildflower meadow of the collective

imagination. Such a long ascent. It always
begins roughly—one moment
undifferentiated dark, the next, vague
hydrangeas and grinning animals
in skin-tight shirts—this rugged transit,
the very fabric of the way we live our lives.

The Beekeeper's Apprentice

You want the mountain to speak
and when it speaks, first accounting
for the daily pressures a mountain must face,
then recounting (as you've been here before)
in its half-bored, half-languid drawl,
how its formative years were spent
alone, with only negative models, valleys
or those weedy, dog-rotten rills,
those ever underachieving foothills,
you suddenly want the flowers to speak.

To believe that one's loneliness flowers
thus ex nihilo–like from a lack
of sympathy would be conversely
like shouting duck-duck, goose-goose
beauteous forms of substance wild
in a twilit suburban alley
and believing that children will come
bearing expectations and glee.

No one you've ever met behaves this way,
so your wanting the flowers to speak
cannot be used as an example of anything
except the business at hand which
being a beekeeper's apprentice
is getting to know how to handle the bees.

If you were the beekeeper, well . . .

to say you know all a man can do with his hands,
to say you've espied a loosed apiary swooning, swooning,
to say farewell my blossom without appearing too needy,

if you were the beekeeper
you'd have come all this way to hear how this too is difficult.

He Who Would Know Art Must First Feel at His Ease

Green transport and colloquial tremor,
the caterpillar's touching way with grass.
Who would know art must first feel his ease—
poor use of a fine violin.

The caterpillar's touching way with grass,
the night of the long knives and other bad times.
I grasp the poor use of a fine violin:
if I can't think at least I can sing.

The night of the long knives, other bad times,
and the shower scene from Hitchcock's *Psycho*—
if I can't think. At the least, I can sing
and given the world, can find an idea

in a scene from a shower. From Hitchcock's psycho
through vision's locked door the Romantic flees
and is given the world. I find an idea:
read substance into the substantive.

Through vision's locked door the Romantic flees
in the interest of a prescient stare,
reads substance into the substantive,
the brow of a voyeur at his labor.

In the interest of a prescient stare,
green transport and colloquial tremor.
The brow of the voyeur at his labor:
who would know art must first feel this ease.

Matthew Confronts the Very Air

It had my name written all over it,
but that was only half the picture

as of a slight profile in abeyance
or composition with vanishing planes

when resonant forks were what we needed
to extract the subject from the static.

The very air was mixed with signals:
turn sharply light then reft at the stop;

there is no joy in this boy's town;
no mud in upper Muddleville.

It seemed a national tragedy at first—
all those unused wildernesses

when the kids in our own neighborhood
didn't have nearly enough to dream.

Later we believed many of these same things
only we employed thinner, clarified languages

once they had become our children
and we hadn't taken the paper in years.

Like an Avant-garde
Classic in Braille

you feel there is something not quite right
about it. An elbow of light? Homo-
sapience? In the past on occasion

you had tried to fix it, to pin
it down, but it always revolved
just far enough out of your orbit
for those efforts to assume the status
of sensible prospects. Bold outlines
formed the near hills. On the hills,

I mean. And this gave to the greens
and to the luscious yellows
a something very useful to do,
which in turn lent a tolerable,
if slightly twisted, shape to your desire

to go on. So why the sudden itch?
Why all this Sisyphean fuss
and bother? Just the way it is,
you say? Well, let me reassure you—

that standard modernist yarn
about what there is and what
we can think about being
two different things like two
sweet peas in a pod

is simply that, a loose thread
loose in box of like threads.

A god-sized box.

A thread-sized thread.

Diary of a Seducer

It is the forbidden garden scene always and it is always now
though now I am a couple of months removed, spirited
away from what he regularly calls "this experience."

The trumpet flowers have arrived, shock-red
honey-sweet and pendant.
And out on The Avenue there is traffic in addition
and fine minds pregnant with increase
in the old family romance way.

What was the name the doctor fashioned? Wish fulfillment?
Lunarlanguagescape? War impact? Impossible!
His voice is the hide-topped gift box in which I rest.

Only yesterday we rode north to watch the foothills
putting on their winter caps.
How remarkable they looked like the twenties in Paris,
part staircase, part fur.

Role Call of Last Requests

I asked for a few more windows
so I was shown into a flourishing of geometry

to personify the chemistry
between haywired and feels-good-enough.

I've always been a sucker for a pretty theory,
swearing by each new way to let streetlight in.

You guessed it: the translucence trick failed.
I had forgotten to mail the bills again.

I requested an extension (surrender denied!)
I applied myself to squeaking by.

I even employed a habit, as D. had suggested,
but the habit was bad in a done-that sort of way,

all Emersonian antinomianism
with none of the skaterboys' native whimsy.

Will you ever forgive me, I asked myself.
I'm still waiting on the reply.

In Contrast to the Actual Infinite

I started out near the fish market
at the pitched and crowded edge of things
where to belong entailed an immense risk,
like learning to stretch out my first thoughts,
to encompass each expectation of ad infinitum
with broad, curvilinear lines
and the auspicious massing of detail.

Spring remained some few weeks off,
stretching sheepishly on the rise.
I could see it in the crocuses, the maudlin
after-the-fact excuses, and in the brown,
blue-gray birds who passed, like parables,
through the leaf-bare branches,
warbling change, change, the promise of change.

Proper names once obsessed me,
the occult power of names and the manner
by which these plots multiplied—via dividing
each immanence from its precise purpose.

I almost said purchase.
Did you hear me?
Heels scudding the slick rockface.
Fingers scratching out a provisional grip.

Recent Titles from Alice James Books

Ruin, Cynthia Cruz
Forth A Raven, Christina Davis
The Pitch, Tom Thompson
Landscapes I & II, Lesle Lewis
Here, Bullet, Brian Turner
The Far Mosque, Kazim Ali
Gloryland, Anne Marie Macari
Polar, Dobby Gibson
Pennyweight Windows: New & Selected Poems, Donald Revell
Matadora, Sarah Gambito
In the Ghost-House Acquainted, Kevin Goodan
The Devotion Field, Claudia Keelan
Into Perfect Spheres Such Holes Are Pierced, Catherine Barnett
Goest, Cole Swensen
Night of a Thousand Blossoms, Frank X. Gaspar
Mister Goodbye Easter Island, Jon Woodward
The Devil's Garden, Adrian Matejka
The Wind, Master Cherry, the Wind, Larissa Szporluk
North True South Bright, Dan Beachy-Quick
My Mojave, Donald Revell
Granted, Mary Szybist
Sails the Wind Left Behind, Alessandra Lynch
Sea Gate, Jocelyn Emerson
An Ordinary Day, Xue Di
The Captain Lands in Paradise, Sarah Manguso
Ladder Music, Ellen Doré Watson
Self and Simulacra, Liz Waldner
Live Feed, Tom Thompson
The Chime, Cort Day
Utopic, Claudia Keelan
Pity the Bathtub Its Forced Embrace of the Human Form, Matthea Harvey
The Arrival of the Future, B.H. Fairchild
The Art of the Lathe, B.H. Fairchild

Alice James Books has been publishing exclusively poetry since 1973. One of the few presses in the country that is run collectively, the cooperative selects manuscripts for publication through both regional and national annual competitions. New regional authors become active members of the cooperative, participating in the editorial decisions of the press. The press, which historically has placed an emphasis on publishing women poets, was named for Alice James, sister of William and Henry, whose fine journal and gift for writing went unrecognized within her lifetime.

Typeset and Designed by Dede Cummings

Printed by Thomson-Shore
on 50% postconsumer recycled paper
processed chlorine-free